THUS SPAKE
SRI RAMA

SO-AFP-288

COMPILED BY

SWAMI SUDDHASATWANANDA

SRI RAMAKRISHNA MATH

PUBLICATION DEPARTMENT
RAMAKRISHNA MATH ROAD
MADRAS-4 (INDIA)

Published by :
© The President,
Sri Ramakrishna Math,
Mylapore, Madras 600 004.

All Rights Reserved
Seventh Impression
VII-21M 6C-6-94
ISBN 81-7120-205-5

Printed in India at
Sri Ramakrishna Math Printing Press,
Mylapore, Madras 600 004.

CONTENTS

PUBLISHER'S NOTE

WE HAVE very great pleasure
in presenting to our readers
'Thus Spake Sri Rama'. Since
the publication of the Thus
Spake series compiled by the
same author, there has been con-
sistent demand to bring out the
sayings of Bhagavan Sri Rama-
chandra in a similar booklet.
Sri Rama is one of the greatest
of incarnations who was ideal
in all respects. These immortal
utterances have been a source
of perennial inspiration to innumerable souls. Here in this
handy beautiful booklet, they
have been collected from the
Valmiki Ramayana,

the Adhyatma Ramayana and the Yogavasishtha Ramayana and suitably arranged so that the readers will find it very easy to go through and draw inspiration from them. This booklet is tenth in the series.

These memorable sayings, though uttered thousands of years ago, have not lost their potency and are still fresh and invigorating.

An invocation and a short life of Bhagavan Sri Rama have been added in the beginning.

We are thankful to Mrs. Malathy Kerala Varma, B.A., who has helped us a lot to collect some of these sayings and to Prof. Biswaranjan Chakravorty for drawing the cover as a token of their devotion to the Lord.

Our labour will be amply rewarded if this booklet is welcomed by our readers as the previous ones.

June 1972.

PUBLISHER

INVOCATION

रामाय रामचन्द्राय रामभद्राय
वेधसे।
रघुनाथाय नाथाय सीतायाः पतये
नमः॥

I bow to Rama, to Rama-
chandra, to Ramabhadra, the
creator, to the Lord of the Raghus,
the Beloved (of Sita) and the
Lord of Sita.

INTRODUCTION:
SRI RAMA

EVERY devout Hindu believes that god Vishnu, the All-Pervading Spirit, appears in an earthly form whenever His presence is needed on earth to remedy great evils and to re-establish religion. It is believed that Sri Rama, the Prince of Ayodhya, was in reality an incarnation of god Vishnu as the seventh advent, and his task then was to rid India from the onslaught and oppression of the Rakshasas, to protect the saints and sages and to show the ideal of a perfect polity.

In Treta Yuga, there reigned

in Ayodhya (U.P.) a noble ruler
named Dasaratha who was not
only a glorious king but a great
hero. His lineage was of the
venerable race of the Sun.
Though Dasaratha had three
devoted wives, Kausalya, Kaikeyi
and Sumitra, he was not blessed
with a son to succeed him to the
throne. So he performed a horse-
sacrifice under the guidance of
the famous sage Rishya-Sringa.
A majestic figure came out of the
flames holding a pot full of
Payasam, which the queens con-
sumed, and in course of time
Sri Rama was born of Kausalya,
Bharata of Kaikeyi and Laks-
mana and Satrughna of Sumitra.
The sons are considered to be the
parts of Lord Vishnu. Rama,

the eldest, was the repository of all divine virtues, and the object of love, affection and reverence of all. All the training prescribed for princes was given to the four brothers. Lakshmana was specially devoted to Rama and Satrughna to Bharata.

When Rama was only sixteen years of age, sage Viswamitra came one day to Ayodhya and asked Dasaratha to send Rama and Lakshmana with him to slay the demons who were creating disturbances and were not allowing the sages to do their sacrificial rites. By the blessing of the sage Viswamitra and by his own powers and skill in archery, Rama killed all the demons. Receiving the blessing of the sages, the brothers were brought to Mithila, the capital of the renowned king Janaka. Here Rama exhibited his wonderful strength and skill by lifting and stringing the wondrous bow of Lord Rudra, which many mighty princes had failed to do. He drew back the bow-string with such a force that the weapon snapped asunder with terrific noise. King Janaka, true to his promise, gave his dearest and lustrous daughter Sita in marriage to Sri Rama.

In course of time Dasaratha became old, and he wanted to install Sri Rama as the crown prince. All arrangements were complete, when all of a sudden the cruel queen Kaikeyi who was ill-advised by her very crooked maid servant Manthara, asked Dasaratha for two boons, which he had once promised. By one boon, Rama should be banished for fourteen years and by the second boon, her own son Bharata should be installed as the crown-prince. Being deeply devoted to father Rama at once retired to the forest, accompanied by Sita and Lakshmana. Unable to bear the rude shock, Dasaratha breathed his last. Bharata who had great reverence and love for Rama tried in vain to bring Rama back, but failing, he ultimately installed Rama's sandals on the throne and started ruling the kingdom in the name of Rama.

Rama, Sita and Lakshmana settled in Panchavati, from where Sita was abducted, by the Rakshasa King of Lanka, Ravana, during the absence of both Rama and Lakshmana, who had been drawn away by the deceptions of a Rakshasa named Maricha. Ravana tried his best to persuade Sita to become his queen, but she was fully absorbed in the thought of Rama and spurned his evil proposal with all the contempt it deserved. Sita was therefore imprisoned in a grove. Rama set out with Lakshmana in hectic search of Sita, got some clue from the dying Jatayu and from the Vanara King Sugriva. He made friends with Sugriva, helped him to destroy his usurping brother Vali and with an army of Vanaras provided by Sugriva, reached Lanka for the rescue of Sita.

A great battle took place between Rama and Ravana, and in the end Ravana, with all his gallant warriors, was killed and Sita was rescued.

But Rama at first refused to accept Sita, as she had so long been confined by Ravana. To prove her innocence, Sita entered fire, and to the unspeakable joy of each and every one, Agni, the god of Fire, came out with Sita, declaring her to be of unsullied purity, and bade Rama take her back as his wife.

Rama's joy knew no bounds and after installing Vibhishana,

the brother of Ravana, on the throne of Lanka, he returned to Ayodhya with Sita, Lakshmana, Vibhishana, Sugriva and Hanuman, the most faithful and devoted Bhakta of Sri Rama. Great were the rejoicings at Ayodhya at the return of Rama after fourteen long years, and Rama along with Sita were crowned by the sage Vasishtha as the King of Ayodhya.

So began the long and prosperous reign of Rama which the bards agree in recording in one voice as the 'Golden Age' of Ayodhya; for they say:

"Untimely death visited not the subjects of Rama. They enjoyed freedom from disease. Women had not to bewail the loss of their husbands or children. No robbers, cheats or false dealers were found anywhere; for each man loved his neighbour as himself. Trees yielded fruits as each season came; harvest never failed to fill the granaries to overflowing; and people were satisfied with the fruits of their labour. Everywhere there was joy, health and happiness."

The immortal sage Valmiki has depicted this divine and wonderful life of Sri Rama in his famous epic Ramayana, which is an eternal companion to all Hindus even today.

*   *   *

"Rama, the ancient idol of the heroic ages, the embodiment of truth, of morality, the ideal son, the ideal husband, the ideal father, and above all, the ideal king, this Rama has been presented before us by the great sage Valmiki. No language can be purer, none chaster, none more beautiful and at the same time simpler than the language in which the great poet has depicted the life of Rama."

— SWAMI VIVEKANANDA.

Thus Spake Sri Rama

PARAMATMAN

SRI Rama tells Hanuman, " It
is the shadow of the Paramatman that you see reflected
in all the living beings as Jivatman. Don't you see the great
sky reflected in each and every
lake or river ? "

The Paramatman is the sky
which is stationary. Its reflections are not permanent. Just
as the sky alone exists, so also
the Paramatman, which is the
Supreme Brahman, is the only
reality. All the visible living

things are only its reflections.

* * *

I am the Paramatman and you are the reflection of Mine. This great secret which I told you just now should never be disclosed to those who have no devotion to Me, even if you are offered a kingdom in exchange. There is no greater advice than this, which I can give you.

* * *

The rope alone is true, the snake is untrue. Similarly, Paramatman alone is real; this world is unreal. The latter appears as real in man's vision, hearing and thoughts, but it lasts only as long as the things seen in a dream last.

Two

The Atman is certainly different from the body, senses, mind and Prana. It is blissful, supreme, non-dual, permanent, formless, sinless and pure. The moment this realisation comes to you, you are liberated.

*   *   *

Try to experience the identity of the Paramatman and the Jivatman by listening to the wise words of your Guru with faith. His advice is, ' Tat Twam Asi ' (Thou art That). Of course the Guru's grace is essential for you to reach that stage.

*   *   *

To be blessed with his grace, first you must understand the meaning of the words Tat Twam

Three

Asi. 'Tat' means 'Paramatman', 'Twam' means 'Jivatman', and 'Asi' means 'are'.
It therefore means that both
Paramatman and Jivatman are
the same. Since both Paramatman and Jivatman are one
and the same, it is not possible to
differentiate them. It is also
impossible to attribute separate
qualities to them.

*   *   *

The body which is made up
of the five elements and which is
limited and perishable, is different from the Atman. Atman is
without beginning and end. It
is indestructible. It creates this
body. Think well over this and
try to know the Atman.

Four

By this process of *Neti Neti* (elimination), you should try to find out what exactly the Atman is. Thus scrutinizing the world which is a mixture of good and evil, take its essence and discard the rest, just as you throw away the seed of a ripe mango after taking its sweet juice. The Atman has no birth or death. It has no childhood, youth or old age.

* * *

The Atman is all-blissful. Why should you think that the miserable Samsara (world) exists in such Atman? It is because of your ignorance that you feel that sorrow exists in the Atman. With the dawn of knowledge, this notion vanishes.

Five

It is by delusion that you feel the existence of something that really does not exist, just as you imagine a snake in a rope. This imagination or false notion that something unreal is real, is what is called Adhyasa (superimposition). The Atman which is Satchidananda (existence-knowledge-bliss) is untouched by such delusion.

* * *

Do you know how the Atman appears as being affected by happiness and misery? Just as a piece of iron which is heated in fire appears to be fire itself, the Atman when reflected in Buddhi, makes us feel that it is affected by joys and sorrows. In fact, the Atman is unaffected.

Six

When you truly understand
that the Atman, which is your
true Self, is without any attribute or attachment, you would
give up your identification with
your body which is inert and
impermanent. So seek the true
nature of the Atman.

*　　　*　　　*

If you constantly think of the
Atman, your mind will be purified and your ignorance will be
up-rooted along with the past
tendencies, just as your ailments
will completely disappear by
your taking medicine daily.
When the mind is pure, you will
get unalloyed bliss.

*　　　*　　　*

How will you think about your

Atman constantly? Vedas advise you to go to a secluded spot, control the senses and without any evil thought, ponder over the Atman only. Thus thinking, you must merge the world in the all-pervading Atman. Then only will you get supreme bliss.

* * *

Think that you are Parabrahman, you have no attachment, you are all-knowing and you are pure. Always feel like this and establish your oneness with the Paramatman and derive bliss within yourself without caring to know what is outside of you. Then you will remain as calm and independent as the sea without the restless waves.

Eight

A yogi who spends his days thinking of the Atman alone has to live until his Prarabdhas are exhausted. After that he will merge in Me, the Paramatman.

*　　　*　　　*

My dear Lakshmana, I disclose to you the greatest secret, namely, the Paramatman, by knowing which the illusion of the world immediately disappears. First I shall give you the description of Maya. After that, I shall explain to you the detailed process of acquiring Jnana. Then I shall tell you about Vijnana and afterwards about Paramatma, by knowing which one does not have fear of anything.

Nine

SELF

THE Self is all-pervading, in-
finite, Satchidananda, and
eternal. It does not possess the
qualities of Buddhi.

*   *   *

It does not undergo transfor-
mation and other Shadbhava
Vikaras (six-fold change). It is
by the Self-illumination of Atma
that the whole universe is illu-
mined. It is one without a
second. It has got attributes of
truth and wisdom. It is unattached. It is the Supreme
Lord, unseen. This Atman can
be known by intuition.

*   *   *

When one realises the truth of unity between Jivatma and Paramatma either by instruction from the Guru or from texts, that very moment the source of ignorance along with the cause and effect will mingle with Paramatma. The state mentioned above is called Moksha. The Self is ever-free.

❖   ❖   ❖

This body is said to be the root of the tree of Samsara. Through this body, the Self comes into contact with sons and other relations. If the body is non-existent, how can there be relations for the Self, which is unattached (Asanga), with sons and relations?

Eleven

DEVOTION

O Sage! I know that your heart has become very pure by your constant thinking of Me. That is why I have come to see you. In order to please Me, you need not do any other Sadhana.

*   *   *

Those who take shelter under Me in this world, meditating on Me and repeating the Mantra of My sacred name, will surely get My vision, even unasked, as I know they have no other refuge.

*   *   *

As a result of the spiritual disciplines you have undergone you are even now liberated from all worldly desires. After your death, you will attain union with Me.

*   *   *

For one who serves the Yogis, who are greatly devoted to Me and who are possessed of pure knowledge and supreme bliss, Mukti is in the palm of his hand.

*   *   *

It does not matter whether you are a man or a woman; your caste, name and position are not taken into account. You might belong to any Ashrama of life. Devotion is the only thing that is essential to worship Me. It is impossible for a person to see Me by the merit of sacrifice, austerity, charity or by the study of the Vedas or by performing the scriptural rites, if he is devoid of devotion to Me.

*

Therefore lady, I shall explain to you briefly the Bhakti Sadhana. Remember that the first discipline to be undergone in this system, is to seek the company of the holy and the virtuous.

*

Just as, even people possessing eyes, cannot see things clearly in the night, but they can see their steps well when a light is brought, so also in those having devotion towards Me, the Self becomes Self-effulgent.

*

Fourteen

The following is the way for cultivating devotion:

Keeping company with My devotees, always serving Me and My Bhaktas, fasting on Ekadasi, celebrating the festivals connected with Me, hearing, reading and expounding My glories, worshipping Me with continuous devotion, and singing of My excellences. If one follows these precepts daily, one gets pure devotion.

* * *

Those that have devotion towards Me will get knowledge and renunciation and they will attain to liberation from the round of births and deaths.

* * *

Those who have no devotion to Me, but jump from Sastra to Sastra in their quest after Truth, only get more and more deluded. Such people can never get the true knowledge, and they cannot be expected to attain to liberation even in the course of hundreds and thousands of births.

*　　　*　　　*

But once you get devotion, you will attain Moksha without any difficulty. By My own command, you will reach the highest goal since you are very much devoted to Me.

*　　　*　　　*

The second thing that you 'd do is to narrate the

Sixteen

accounts of My cosmic activities and the third is enumerating My various good qualities. Pondering over and explaining My words and instructions in detail is the fourth sadhana. Seeking a Guru and acquiring good habits by self-control and observing laws should be the fifth discipline to be practised.

*   *   *

As the sixth, you must worship Me very regularly and the seventh should be receiving a sacred mantra of Mine from your Guru. Worshipping My devotees by all means and seeing everything as Me is the eighth sadhana and non-attachment to anything else is the ninth. This is the nine-fold path of Bhakti.

Seventeen

By following this path of devotion Mukti comes to anyone, whether one is a man or woman of low or high birth. Devotion means universal love. When you get devotion then my Tattwas become clear to you. He who realises Me gets liberation in this birth itself.

* * *

Thus devotion becomes the means to attain Moksha. This is certain. If you begin with the first Sadhana, then all others will follow in course of time. Bhakti and Mukti are assured for you since you are My devotee. I have come to you. By My darshan you will attain Mukti, you need not fear at all.

Eighteen

This world has no separate existence; it exists only in our imagination just as we imagine the existence of a snake in the rope.

*   *   *

When you are able to know the Paramatman by the process of 'Neti' 'Neti', then only you can give up all work; until then you have to carry on doing your duties. The moment the realisation comes that Atman is different from the body, senses etc., delusion (Maya) which is the root cause of Samsara, is destroyed.

*   *   *

How can this Maya, which is full of tendencies (Vāsanās), be killed by mere arguments and study of the Srutis? It is never possible. Only by gaining supreme knowledge can it be destroyed, after which there is no fear of its return.

* * *

The Idea that "I am this body" is ignorance (Avidya), which is the mother of delusion. "I am not the body. I am Atman" —this realisation is knowledge (Vidya), which is the destroyer of delusion. Avidya is the cause of Samsara and Vidya is the destroyer of Samsara. Therefore, those who want to attain liberation should work with one-pointed attention to gain this knowledge.

* * *

In this effort, man will have to face many enemies like 'Kama' or desire, 'Krodha' or anger, 'Lobha' or greed, and 'Moha' or delusion. Of these, anger is the most fearful foe who will try to put all sorts of obstacles in one's struggle to attain liberation.

*　　　*　　　*

Prompted by anger man kills his own mother, father, brother, friends and relations. He will often have occasion to repent of actions done under the impulse of anger. It is anger that binds him to Samsara. Anger it is that destroys one's virtues. So give up anger. Anger indeed is Yama, the great enemy, and greed is the river Vaitharini which is very difficult to cross. Contentment is Nandana Vana (heavenly garden) and peace (Shanti) is Kamadhenu (heavenly cow of plenty). Ponder over it and crave for peace.

*　　　*　　　*

If you have patience, then you will never have any enemy. Atman is different from the body, senses, mind, intelligence and life. It is pure, self-effulgent, blissful, devoid of emotions and is formless. As long as you do not consider the Atman as different from the body, senses and life, you will be afflicted by the sorrows of this world like disease, death etc.

Twenty six

MIND AND BODY

O sage, lust is like a huge tree. It is covered with the creeper of desire. It has got innumerable branches. The mind that roams over them can never get the desired fruit.

* * *

I clearly see that such men are rare who do not become dejected when faced with danger, or overcome by delusion, who do not become proud when their selfish end is attained and who are not perturbed by the glances of women. We can seldom find such men.

* * *

The mind is never satisfied

even when it has an object of desire in its grasp, just as a pot that leaks is never filled with any quantity of water.

*　　　　*　　　　*

The mind cherishing ambition remains always empty. That is why it finds rest nowhere like a deer that has lost track of the herd.

*　　　　*　　　　*

The tendencies of the mind are always restless like waves. Failing to free itself from that restlessness, it cannot achieve composure even for a moment. Agitated by the pursuit of the object of senses, it runs in various directions.

*　　　　*　　　　*

Twenty eight

This ghost of a mind is absolutely devoid of existence. It assumes a shape only through vain imagination. Again its non-existence is realised by discrimination. To control this ghost is extremely difficult.

*   *

The mind burns one more than fire, and it is harder than Vajra. It runs after an object of sense like the crow after meat, and the next moment it gives it up like a child. It cannot stick to anything whatsoever.

*   *   *

The mind, like an eddying sea, carries man afar. To check the mind is more difficult than desiccating the ocean, uprooting the mountain or eating fire.

Twenty nine

This body is composed of the five gross elements (earth, water, fire, air and ether), the five Tanmatras or rudimentary elements (sound, touch, form, taste and smell), intelligence, five organs of knowledge and five organs of action.

*   *   *

The leaf that is this body takes no time in yellowing and dropping down on the ground. This body has its origin in false knowledge. So it is full of delusions like a dream. The transitoriness of this body is obvious.

*   *   *

Old age in the forest of the body is like a she-jackal with her hideous cry than which a more

Thirty

ominous sound is never heard on earth. If the sense-organs are taken as children, these children cannot freely play in the house of the body dampened by old age.

*   *   *

No man was ever born who could conquer old age which causes every single desire of his to remain unfulfilled. As darkness follows sunset, death follows old age.

*   *   *

After a scrutiny of things inside and outside this body, just tell Me, O sage, if you find anything good in it. How can one have any reliance on this body

which does not go along with
one when one dies?

*   *   *

The childhood is spent in fun
and frolic; the mind remains
absolutely restless at that time.
In youth man runs after sensual
pleasure and can never expect
to get peace. And in old age,
the body becomes diseased and
starts decaying. At this stage,
man experiences nothing but
sorrow.

*   *   *

As the bee leaves the lotus
dried up due to snow fall, so also
when this body is attacked with
fell disease and old age, the bee
of life leaves it, and the lake of

Thirty two

the world becomes completely dried.

*   *   *

This fragile and changeable body with its complexities of the entrails and the nerves—this too is a prolific source of sorrows.

*   *   *

In spite of its materiality, the body has the semblance of consciousness owing to its being inhabited by the Atman with its five sheaths.

*   *   *

The dwelling place of the infatuated soul, this body, incapable of discriminating between permanence and evanescence, serves only to throw men into the pit of ignorance. The slightest

Thirty three

provocation will suffice to fill it with joy or suffuse it with tears. Hence, nothing can be found so contemptible, lamentable and so utterly devoid of good points as the body.

*   *   *

Its ephemerality notwithstanding, the body has the capacity of helping in the achievement of liberation (Moksha). That is why the body is not like an ordinary material substance, nor is it wholly a conscious entity.

*   *   *

The vulture of egoism, the serpent of longings, the raven of anger and the birds of the senses live here in this tree of the body. Over and above all, the various

Thirty four

desires have formed themselves into rows of thick entangled masses around the foot of this tree.

* * *

The body is like a tortoise that lies inactive in the pit of longings without making an effort for release.

* * *

Many many are the bodies floating adrift in the ocean of this world. Amongst these, some particular bodies, receptive to knowledge and discrimination, are called human bodies.

* * *

Superior indeed is the person who can attain peace by deciding thus: I have no relations with the body; this body and I are not identical.

Thirty five

YOUTH

IGNORANT youth falls a prey to various playful propensities of the restless mind and is thrown from sorrow to sorrow. The demon of lust residing in the pit of the heart, brings under its sway the young man who loses self-control.

* * *

That man rightly deserves the appellation of the tranquil one, who has safely crossed the terrible forest of youth so full of curious incidents.

* * *

It would be easier to cross a turbulent river than to relinquish the longings of youth.

Thirty six

Youth is the cause of degradation of one who is devoid of discrimination.

*　　　*　　　*

As a gem vanishes from the grip of an ill-starred person, the bird of youth flies away from the body in no time.

*　　　*　　　* .

'A brute of a man' is the fittest description of a person who is elated and fascinated by youth that lasts not.

*　　　*　　　*

O Sadhu, only they are to be reverenced and only they deserve to be called men, who have crossed the crisis of youth with ease.

Thirty seven

To cross an ocean infested with crocodiles would be found easy when compared with passing through the period of youth so full of evil and swelling currents of lust.

*　　　*　　　*

O Sage, the youth that is adorned with humility and brightened by qualities like kindness, is youth beautiful. In this world, a youth of that description is very rare to find indeed.

*　　　*　　　*

Like frost destroying the lotus, and the river destroying the trees on its banks, decrepitude makes an end of youth. To what ugliness does age reduce the body

Thirty eight

of man, playing havoc with his limbs!

* * *

The Goddess of wealth is as restless as the waves. She does not stay with any one for ever. So also, youth is very short. The pleasures that you get by enjoying a woman is just like a dream. Your lifetime is so little.

* * *

LIFE AND INEVITABLE END

LIKE drops of water hanging from the tip of a leaf, the life of a man leaves this dirty body all of a sudden.

*   *   *

Life is the cause of sorrow to those who have not developed the power of discrimination and whose heart is oppressed owing to contact with the serpent of sense objects.

*   *   *

On the contrary, life means happiness to those who have found peace in the knowledge of Reality.

*   *   *

This our life is evanescent like the clouds of autumn; it is like the lamp of which the oil has been exhausted; it is like the ripple on a sheet of water.

*   *   *

Despite this hollowness of life, fools desire longevity. But that brings only sorrow in its train.

*   *   *

Just as the mice burrow into the earth inch by inch everyday, time takes away the lives of living beings minute by minute.

*   *   *

Like the cat keenly watching the mouse, death keeps watch on the life of every one.

*   *   *

Forty one

The ignorant man thinks that as far as he is concerned, night and day will come and go till eternity. Immersed in sense enjoyments, he does not see the march of time.

*   *   *

Like the water contained in an unburnt pot, man's life is getting extinguished every second.

Enemies like diseases catch-hold of man's body and destroys it. Old age like a tigress jumps upon it and attacks it. Death is always watching when to come and take possession of it.

*   *   *

Life is evanescent, but fools take it to be real and they get

Forty two

entangled in it. The sun comes and goes every day; our lifetime also is getting shorter and shorter along with that. Even by witnessing the old age and death of others, no one realises that it is going to be his fate also

*　　　　*　　　　*

All accumulation comes to an end by depletion. Elevations end by crumbling and falling. Unions end by separation. Life ends by death.

*　　　　*　　　　*

As ripe fruits must inevitably fall to the ground, so must a man, once he is born on earth, inevitably perish.

*　　　　*　　　　*

Just as a building supported by strong pillars decays in course of time and comes down, so do men pass away, being victims of old age and death.

*   *   *

The night that passes away, never returns. The Ganges discharges her waters into the great ocean but never turns back in her course.

*   *   *

Days and nights pass over the heads of all creatures on earth and soon consume their lives as the sun's rays dry up the water in summer.

*   *   *

Whether you stand still or move, your days diminish. Grieve,

Forty four

then, for yourself. Why grieve for aught else?

* * *

Death travels with one; death rests with one. However far one goes, one cannot leave death behind.

* * *

The skin is wrapt in folds and wrinkles. The hairs turn white. Age destroys a man. What can he do to avoid this?

* * *

At sunrise men rejoice thinking they may work and earn. At sunset they rejoice also thinking they can enjoy themselves. But they do not realise that their lives are shrinking.

* *

Forty five

As the seasons come round, men fancy they will ever be fresh and feel happy. But with each cycle of the seasons, our lives are shortened.

*　　　*　　　*

As logs of wood come together on the wide ocean, and having drifted together for a time, part from one another, so do wives, sons, kinsmen and possessions come together, and separate. This separation is unavoidable.

*　　　*　　　*

No one on earth ever escapes the course of nature. So mourning for the dead is of no avail. Nor can one escape when one's turn comes.

*　　　*　　　*

As a man falling in with a caravan on the move, says to those there, " I too will accompany you ", so is the journey of life, which has been already performed by our fathers and grandfathers. If one joins the journey, which knows no change, how can one complain ?

*   *   *

Life is a stream that never reverses its course, so one's life ever lessens in duration.

WORLD AND WEALTH

IN the world, good company is difficult to find, and truth is manifest nowhere. The mind is darkened by ignorance, and the qualities like friendliness and joy are not in evidence. Only depravity finds a rich soil in this world.

*　　　*　　　*

In this world people are born to die and they die to be born again. All these things of enjoyment are evanescent and are the roots of sins and dangers. The mutual relations of the objects of senses are mere figments of imagination. The world is as it is presented in the mind, and the mind appears to be without existence.

*　　　*　　　*

I am sad at heart pondering over the ways and means as to how to remove these causes of grief. The thought of the sorrows of this world has made my heart bleak and dreary like a cremation ground. Thinking of the transience and other varied demerits of the world, I am restless like a wild elephant in chains.

*　　　*　　　*

Can a seeker after truth find his sole satisfaction in such a cavern of sense enjoyments? Time swallows them up, who think that they find happiness in such a world.

The world that is before us is fleeting like a dream. The mountain ranges that kiss the clouds today may within a short lapse of time be reduced to a plain stretch of land.

*　　　*　　　*

Everything in this world has to undergo changes—even childhood, youth and old age in the case of embodied beings. Everything is passing from state to state like waves.

*　　　*　　　*

Every single day sees the destruction of things as well as their generation; but this cursed world never comes to a close. Men are reborn as animals, the lower animals are again born as men;

Fifty

the gods are demoted. So where shall we look for permanence in this world?

*　　　　*　　　　*

The beauties of nature are as impermanent as flashes of lightning. All creatures, even Brahma, Vishnu and Rudra, are rushing towards annihilation like the waters that flow into a desert.

*　　　　*　　　　*

Possessions and enjoyments are the root of all anxieties; far better is the cultivation of the equable temperament in seclusion unperturbed by any thought.

*　　　　*　　　　*

The objects of sense enjoyment are the real poison, and

not what is popularly known as poison. For the so-called poison destroys the body in one birth, while the poison of sense enjoyments hurts man from birth to birth through a countless series of embodiments.

* * *

The world is transitory, having not a grain of happiness in it. I do not desire death nor do I covet life; I have no eagerness for kingdom, wealth, enjoyments and desires, for I have relinquished egoism which is the root of all these.

* * *

It is true that the world is apparently beautiful but in its true nature, it is very ugly. In this world, everything ends in sorrow. Nothing in this world can afford real peace to the mind.

* * *

Just as a river produces a series of swirling waves during the rains, wealth too whirls the foolish men into eddies of pride and haughtiness.

* * *

As the billows are born of the stream, worries without number are born of wealth. It causes man to be as restless as the billows, and prompts him to perpetrate evil deeds.

* * *

As a gem covered with ashes becomes dirty, so also scholars,

Fifty three

heroes, humble and grateful persons lose their respective nature and become corrupted when they amass wealth.

* * *

As the poisonous creeper becomes the cause of death, so also worldly property brings only sorrow instead of happiness. There is possibility of losing the self if a man spends all his energy only to preserve his property.

* * *

The fool feels in his heart that wealth is the highest good and the only way to happiness. In reality, it causes ignorance, sorrow and all untoward circumstances.

* * *

Just as the dust tarnishes even the brightness of a gem, wealth too contaminates the virtues of the wise.

＊　　　　＊　　　　＊

Lakshmi charms the imagination of men with fleeting colours as of a rainbow; she is restless like the lightning.

TIME

AEONS after aeons pass, and
the flux that is called Time
remains unaffected and steady.
Time has therefore neither rise,
nor movement, nor a static con-
dition.

*   *   *

Time again is the moon for the
lotus of man's youth, and a lion
to the elephant of men's span of
life. There is nothing to be
found on earth, big or small,
which Time does not make an
end of.

*   *   *

With no device of the intellect
could man penetrate the mystery
of Time. For, in the whole

world of life, Time is the most patent entity.

* * *

Just as fire burns the abode of men, Time burns men by rousing various ambitions in their hearts. This tyrant of Time has no compassion even for one who is laden with sorrow.

* * *

O Sage, what ignorant people take for an abode of enjoyment, is in fact a receptacle of pangs: life is fleeting, youth short-lived, childhood darkened by lack of intellect, and death terrible.

* * *

There is no entity in this world which does not fall a prey to this all-swallowing Time. Time is very terrible. Time swallows up

Fifty seven

everything that is visible, sparing nothing. It does not spare even outstanding personalities.

*   *   *

Time which is collossal in its dimensions, brings a thing into being in a trice and breaks it to pieces in a moment. Time recurrently shifts, from heaven to hell and back, a creature which identifies itself with its body.

*   *   *

Time devours everything. Man's ill luck and good fortune, restlessness and composure, greed and infatuation—everything resides in the womb of Time.

*   *   *

From a blade of grass and particle of dust to the oceans and the Sumeru and even Indra

Fifty eight

himself—all are subject to the mercy of Time.

*　　　*　　　*

Causing the rain and the moon to rise and set in this firmament, Time plays, as it were, with them in the fashion of a boy with his ball.

*　　　*　　　*

The ocean produces and destroys a series of waves in a single operation. Likewise Time maintains on its bosom the flux of creation—originating our species now, destroying it next moment, and creating another, endlessly. The numberless worlds are like falling figs, the innumerable living things are like mosquitoes and Time is like the fig tree that bears the figs.

Fifty nine

ADVICE TO
LAKSHMANA

O Lakshmana! Hear what I tell you as to how you can know this Jiva. Paramatman and Jivatman are the two names of the one self-same thing. There is no difference between the two.

* * *

Only the ignorant think that they are different. You should give up pride, egoism, wickedness and crookedness. You should never care for the criticism of others.

* * *

Neither should you find fault with any one. Control your mind, speech and body, and never be perturbed. Daily do service to your Guru with devotion after purifying your body and mind. Do not be slack in doing good actions even for a single day.

* * *

Do not give up truth. Be always cheerful. The thought of enjoying the senses should immediately be controlled. Thinking that birth, old age and death are your lot, be always humble. Do not have intense love or attachment to your wife and children.

* * *

You should avoid mixing with crowds as far as possible. Stay in a pure secluded place and do not keep company with crooked people. Try to live all alone, eager to know the Paramatman by searching into the Vedas and Vedantas and their commentaries, and doing all the Vedic rites.

*   *   *

Do not be overjoyed if you get a fortune, neither should you be dejected if you lose it. Your mind should be well balanced. I, Rama, is the life of all souls. Your mind should be fixed on Me alone.

*   *   *

Thus, you will get the realisation in your mind that you are the ever pure Chidatman who is different from the senses, attributes and forms. When you gain this, then I think you have

Sixty two

gained supreme knowledge. You will be able to experience this yourself in your life, namely, that Atman is not the body, breath, intelligence or this ego.

* * *

The Atman has no emotions and qualities, but it is supreme bliss itself. It has no beginning and no end. It is all-pervading, indivisible, one, non-dual, supreme, devoid of qualities, filling the whole universe, and formless. It is the paramount truth, not to be measured by one's intelligence or knowledge and it is untouched by Maya.

* * *

To experience this directly you should seek the help of a Guru who will explain this to you from the Sastras. When you experience that you and every other Jiva are none other than the Paramatman itself, then you gain Mukti (Salvation). Without Jnana, Vijnana and Vairagya, it is not possible to attain Mukti. And one who has got it is very rare in this world.

*　　　*　　　*

For attaining this state, devotion to Me is most important. Even if you have got eyes, you need a light to see your steps in darkness. In the same way, even if you have enough knowledge, you need devotion to Sri Rama in order to see the right path.

*　　　*　　　*

Sixty four

If you have it, then what more do you want? My Bhakta will get Jnana, Vijnana and Vairagya automatically. The sages say like this. Thus at your request I have explained to you the way of salvation (Mukti Marga). Whosoever digests this properly and follows it, will attain liberation.

* * *

Since you are dear to me, I have told you this. Whosoever thinks over this advice of Mine and acts accordingly, is really a wise man. He will be liberated from all sins. O brother! witnessing this whole world as being pervaded by Me, serve Me with great faith. You will thus be pure, happy, blissful and healthy.

Sixty five

Whoever serves Me at least once, mentally regarding Me as Saguna (with attributes) as well as Nirguna (without attributes), will be purified by the sacred dust of My feet, as the three worlds are purified by the rays of the sun. This advice is not insignificant. This is the essence of all that is said in the Srutis.

*   *   *

What I have advised you is the knowledge that can be obtained only by the study of Vedanta. He who studies this with great faith and devotion to Me and My words, will surely attain union with Me.

*   *   *

MISCELLANEOUS

AS long as I live, I cannot violate the promise given to the ascetics. I may give up my life or even Sita as well as Lakshmana, but I cannot be false to a vow made to a devotee.

* * *

Our predicament is not different from that of the deer that runs from horizon to horizon in search of water led on by the sight of mirage at a distance. Even while perfectly aware of the deception of the senses, we are like fools behaving like their slaves.

* * *

Smiles and tears, decrepitude

and death eternally recur. Our lot is to pine away like a cluster of plants battered by random gusts of wind, and all this is due to the object of enjoyments of no worth. Men, devoid of intelligence, fail to realise this position.

*   *   *

These worldly enjoyments are as fleeting as the streak of lightning emerging from the clouds.

*   *   *

As long as you identify yourself with this body you will feel miserable. Atman is not the body, sense or ego. It is due to ignorance that you are affected by these worldly sorrows.

*   *   *

When you dream of something, it seems real as long as the dream lasts. Similarly, to a man who always thinks of the senses and the pleasures derived therefrom, this world seems real.

*　　　*　　　*

He plunges into Samsara to gain his own selfish ends. It is full of hatred, greed, jealousy etc. Mind is the creator of Samsara, and again it is mind that binds you to it.

*　　　*　　　*

Hatred should cease along with the other one's death. You should never hate a dead man.

*　　　*　　　*

If a man comes as a friend, how can I reject him? It is

against the law of my life. Once a man surrenders himself, one should overlook all his faults.

* * *

When someone comes to me for refuge, I cannot disappoint him. This is my dharma. It does not matter if as a result I suffer. Even at the cost of my life, I must do this duty of mine. Never can I deviate from this.

* * *

Verily I tell you, even if Ravana himself came to me for sanctuary, I would accept him without hesitation.

* * *

It is a heinous crime not to give shelter to those who petition for it. One will be deprived of

Seventy

heaven and glory as also of one's strength and powers, if shelter is denied to him who surrenders.

* * *

A person who pursues the path of duty should regard his elder brother, the one who has begotten him, and the one who instructs him in wisdom, as his three fathers.

* * *

Righteousness demands that a younger brother, a son and a virtuous disciple should be regarded as one's own offspring.

* * *

Even for the virtuous, duty is subtle and not easy to grasp; the soul residing in the heart alone knows what is right and what is wrong.

Seventy one

So be always calm and sinless and meditate on me daily. You will be rescued from this dreadful sea of Samsara.

* * *

Timely doing of good actions and obeying the age-old laws, are especially necessary to gain Mukti.

* * *

But if these good deeds are done with a sense of ego, they only bind you to this world. So to gain knowledge you should work without the least trace of pride.

* * *

Pure knowledge is that which kills all desires and attachments. Any work with a particular motive behind it should be given up, it only binds you to the cycle of birth and death. It is harmful for your attaining real knowledge.

* * *

Like the fowler spreading his net, egoism creates various fascinating illusions in the minds of men. Terrible grief arises from egoism. It is the Rahu for the moon of peace; it is like frost for a bed of lotuses.

* * *

As long as a man is egotistical, he is bound to suffer. And when there is no egoism, there is no suffering. So the best course is to remain without egoism.

* * *

It is egoism that has spread the net of attachment for the wife and children—a net out of which no magical spell will bring escape. So all mental pain automatically vanishes when egoism is eschewed.

* * *

Rama to Kaikeyi:

O Mother: Why do you say thus to me? I am prepared to give up even my life for the sake of my father. I can drink deadly poison to serve him. I will renounce the kingdom, Sita or Mother Kausalya for his sake.

* * *

Discharge of Swadharma (duties allotted to you) is only a Sadhana, means to an end,

Seventy four

namely, gaining Atmajnana. It is not an end in itself.

* * *

Therefore always meditate upon the Atman on the lotus of your heart, realising that it is something other than intelligence, senses etc. Then you will not be sorry. Bear all the Prarabdhas that are allotted to you, whether it is happiness or misery.

* * *

Doing your work as if being carried away by the current, you will not become attached to it. Whatever work you do outwardly, O Raghava, let your mind and character be pure.

* * *

Seventy five

The worldly-minded attain the company of the holy saints and sages by the effect of their merits earned by them in their previous births.

* * *

Man does not give up pride. With our mind we always create misery and fear but it is all like a dream. The magic performed by a magician is, as everybody knows, utterly false.

* * *

I (Iswara) view everyone equally. No particular person is very dear to me, and no one is hated by me also. Like the Kalpaka tree, I give whatever is requested of me.

* * *